Great Landmarks

CW00726418

Contents

Written by Vaishali Batra

Introduction

Landmarks stand out from what is around them.
Some landmarks are natural, such as mountains.
Some landmarks are built by people.
This book is about built landmarks.
These are often called **monuments**.
They often stand for something, or are **symbols**.
They may honour great people or events.
There are many built landmarks in the world.

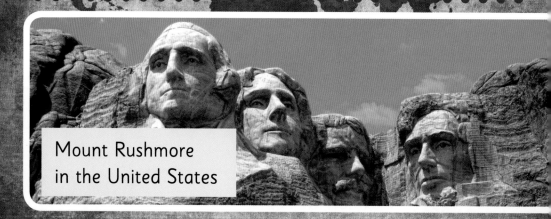

Mount Rushmore
in the United States

The Sydney Opera House in Australia

The Sydney Opera House

The Sydney Opera House
is a great landmark of Australia.
It stands on a point of land where ships
come in and anchor, the **harbour**.
The building is famous for its unique style,
or **design**.
It looks like white sails.

The roof of the Opera House looks like the sails of a ship.

The building's design is unique.

There was a big competition
to find the best design.
Entries came from all around the world.
The winning design was from Denmark.
Construction began in 1959.

The Sydney Opera House is an arts centre.
It has many great theatres.
Concerts and plays are held there.
Dances and operas are performed there, too.

Concerts are held
in this beautiful concert hall.

Building the roof took a long time.

The finished Opera House, seen from the water

The Great Wall of China

The Great Wall is the longest wall in the world.
It is thousands of miles long.
It runs along the northern edge, or **border**,
of China.

Long ago, China had enemies across this border.
Rulers wanted to keep the border safe.
They started to build walls
more than 2,000 years ago.
For a very long time, the walls joined up.
There are forts and watchtowers
all along the wall.

People built the wall to protect China from an invasion from the north.

The wall crosses mountains and plains.
Many people visit this great landmark.
It has become a symbol of China.

Watchtowers along the wall
served as lookout posts.

The wall snakes across the countryside for thousands of miles.

Mount Rushmore

Mount Rushmore is a special landmark
in the United States.
It honours four great presidents.
It helps us remember these people from the past.
A landmark that does this
is called a **memorial**.

The Presidents at Mount Rushmore

Theodore Roosevelt

Abraham Lincoln

George Washington

Thomas Jefferson

Mount Rushmore is
an American memorial.

MOUNT RUSHMORE NATIONAL MEMORIAL

Around 400 men worked on the memorial.
They shaped the rock with dynamite.
They carved the faces
with chisels and hammers.
Work started in 1927 and finished in 1941.
Many tourists go to see this great landmark.
It is a famous symbol of the US.

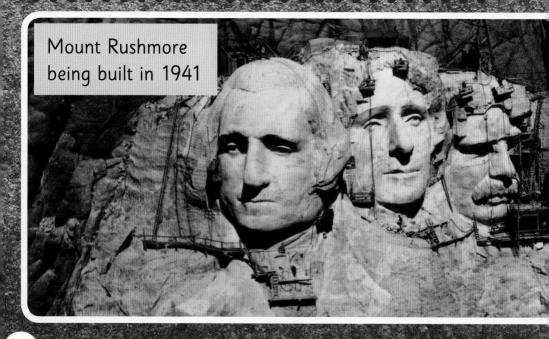

Mount Rushmore
being built in 1941

Many tourists visit this famous landmark.

Each face is about as tall as a six-storey building.

The Statue of Liberty

The Statue of Liberty is also a famous
US monument.
The robed woman is a symbol of freedom.
In one hand, she holds up a torch.
In her other hand, she holds a book.
The book shows the date that the US
became a free country.

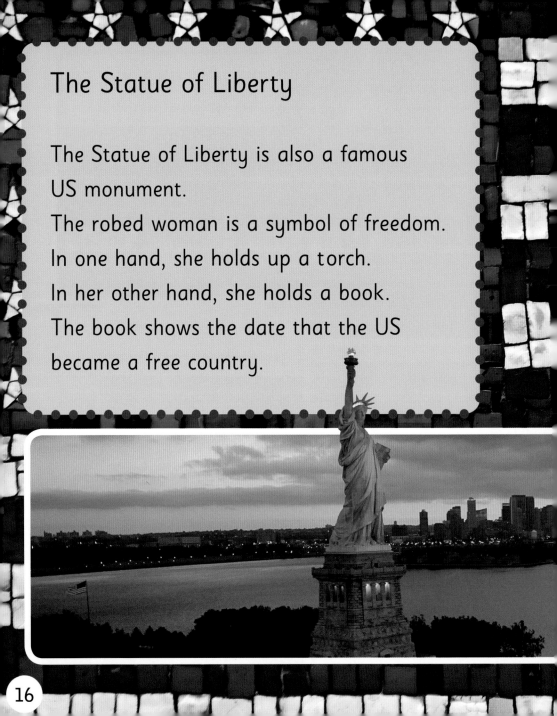

There is an
observation deck
in the crown.

The statue is
a symbol of freedom.

The statue stands in New York Harbour.
In the past, many people
came to New York Harbour on ships.
This monument was their first sight
of a great new land.

The statue was a gift from France to the US.
This was more than 100 years ago.
At the time, it was the tallest landmark
in New York.
People can still see it for miles around.

This painting shows the Statue of Liberty being built in Paris, France.

The Taj Mahal

The Taj Mahal is India's most famous landmark.
It was built more than 400 years ago.
A ruler's beloved wife had died.
He had the Taj Mahal built
as a memorial to her.
She is buried inside.

For many years, thousands of people
worked on the buildings.
Workers came from all around Asia and beyond.

The Taj Mahal is in Agra, northern India.

The main building is made of white marble.
Patterns on the walls
are made with precious gems.
The buildings are near a river.
They are set in beautiful gardens.

There are decorations covering
the inside and outside of the Taj Mahal.

Glossary

border – the edge of a country where it meets other countries

design – the style or shape of something that is made

harbour – a place where ships sail in and anchor

memorial – something built in memory of people or events

monuments – large statues or buildings in honour of a person or event

symbols – things that stand for other things

Index